I CLIMBED OUT OF THE BELLY OF THE BEAST

JOANNA SIRAVO-HAMRIC

Copyright © 2020

Joanna Siravo-Hamric

I Climbed Out Of The Belly Of The Beast

All rights reserved. No part of this publication may be reproduced, distributed, or transmitted in any form or by any means, including photocopying, recording, or other electronic or mechanical methods, without the prior written permission of the publisher, except in the case of brief quotations embodied in critical reviews and certain other non-commercial uses permitted by copyright law.

JOANNA SIRAVO-HAMRIC BRC PUBLISHING

Phoenix, Arizona

For publishing information, please contact

BRC Publishing at drbcombs@gmail.com

Printed in the United States of America

First Printing 2020

First Edition 2020

10 9 8 7 6 5 4 3 2 1

DEDICATION

I dedicate this memoir to my Sons, Derrick, Deon and Derron as I have called them their entire life "my three kings," my Husband, best friend and soul mate, Kevin– May I continue to make you proud. Kim and Ginny for giving me the guidance to try recovery and stick with it. Terri, Doug, Kirstin and Martha for believing in me and encouraging me in the real estate business. Most of all I thank God for giving me another chance at life and to share my experience, strength and hope. I pray that someone will read this and know "I can recover too."

ACKNOWLEDGMENTS

To my family friends, neighbors and co-workers keep the faith. I love you. To my family and friends who are no longer here, Rest In

Paradise: James Hampton, Father, Renaldo Hudson, Nephew Elnora Turner, Mother Olivia Turner, Sister, Charlie and Mary Davis, Grandparents, Anthony Turner Sr, Nephew, Tatiana Turner, Great Niece, Deneen Turner, Niece, DaShan Hudson, Niece, Mischa Taylor, Friend, Darryl (DoWell) Turner Nephew and Melvin Phillips, Friend.

Table Of Contents

Chapter 1: Once Upon A Time 1

Chapter 2: Too Young To Marry 8

Chapter 3: Moving Without A Purpose 13

Chapter 4: Recovery Is Possible 19

Chapter 5: New Life 26

Chapter 6: Finding My Niche 34

Chapter 7: My Testimony 40

About The Author 70

CHAPTER 1

ONCE UPON A TIME

As I began my testimony, my memoir I want to say I never imagine being where I am today. I realize that it is only by the grace of God that I am here to tell you what you are about to read. There is so much that I don't remember but I am going to do my best to show my life as a "open book" as much as I can without harming others including myself.` Being molested as a child, having the feeling of fear constantly surrounding me, hoping that the pain would stop, doing whatever I had to do to survive, today life is so much different. I can face myself today and know I am blessed.

When and where I was born and raised, I knew nothing about race, color, creed or nationality the area was called "Jew Town. Jew Town a variety of shopping, clothing, furniture, thrift shops you name the merchandise you could find it in Jew Town. Jew Town was called Jew Town because Jewish people owned most of the stores in this area during the 1800's.Jew Town was and still is famous for the hot dog stands that sell the best tasting polish, hot dogs, pork chops grilled to perfection with greasy grilled onions as condiments. I was born in Cook County Hospital Ward 41 in Chicago Illinois. My Mom had two daughters; Earlene and

Olivia ages 13 and 14. When I was born, I was a surprise to all. My Dad had one son, Jack and 4 daughters Anne, Eula, Marie and Helen. One of my stepsisters was just a few years younger than my Mom. I don't remember much about my stepsisters and stepbrother except for one, my Dad's youngest daughter, Helen who really did treat me like her sister. She was a beautician and she did not live far from us so I would go to her house and she would do my hair. My Dad had little education. He leased a Checker Cab, numbers runner, and in later years he and my brother in law Bud, owned a vegetable and fruit truck. In the 1960's this was a known business for African American Men. My Dad was a hard worker while he was living, and my Mom did not work outside of the home. Our house was always spotless with meals ready breakfast, lunch and dinner.

In 1956 my family moved to 1646 W 13th St in Chicago. This area was called "Across Ashland." Ashland Ave divided the housing projects from the what was considered at that time the middle-class homes. There was not anything different except one side of Ashland Ave was Chicago public housing and the other side was regular homes and that is where I lived. On our block everyone knew each other, and all the children played with each other. I have a friend Diane; we have been friends since I was around 3 years old and she was 4 years old. Diane and I are still friends today. Diane relocated to Arizona in 2019. Diane's Mom, Miss Anna and my Momma where good friends. My Mother's sister Rosie Lee and her children, Ora (we called her Pee Wee because she was short), Robert, Otis and Charles also lived on the block. During the summer we would all play games in the playground which was directly across the street from my house or play in the streets. We played, red light green light, red rover and Simon says. Those were the good old days!

My relationship with my Dad was special. He always did things to make me feel wanted like when he was driving, he would put me on his lap, and I would pretend I was driving his car. My Dad and I were close, and I feel it was because when I was born my Dad was 59 years old. The love I felt from my Dad was priceless, he called me "shoe shoe baby." He would go to work in the morning, and I would wait for him to return home. I would sit on the stairs waiting patiently for my Dad. As soon as his car was in view I would start crying and he would say "what's wrong with my baby who did something to you"? There was nothing wrong with me, I was just a spoiled brat. When he would drive up and get out of his car, I would run up to him and jump into his arms. On weekends my Dad would drink, and I would drink from his beer cans and he would laugh and say, "Look at my baby acting like me." Today I realize that was not funny and I believe it only added to my addiction later in life because at an incredibly young age I loved the taste of alcohol.

Around age of 3 or 4 is when the sexual abuse started, I was molested by a relative, my older cousin, and never told anyone. This lasted for a few years. I did not tell anyone because he told me if I said anything, he would kill my mother and father. That terrified me to the point that I felt he would do it. He would have me lay across a foot stole face down, he never penetrated me, but he would put his penis between my legs and ejaculate. For years after I felt it was my fault that this happened. Realizing later that the person was sick and I was not the blame for someone else's actions. I carried that guilt into my teen years where I started smoking pot and drinking.

When I was 4 years old one of my sisters, Olivia gave birth to my oldest niece, Debra. For a long time, I thought that Debra was my sister because she lived with my Mom, Dad and me. My Mom's parents also lived with us. The following year my older sister, Earlene gave birth to her first child a girl, Pam. I always had a close relationship with my nieces and nephews because we were so close in age. I had cousins that were my age or older that lived in the same neighborhood as well. At age 5 I attended Kindergarten at Ethan Allen Elementary which was located directly across the street from my home. I was breast fed from birth until I was 6 years old. I would leave school during recess to go home and get breast fed and then go back to school. Eventually my teacher, Miss Bush noticed me doing this and called my Mom. Miss Bush told my Mom that behavior was not acceptable, and it needed to stop; it did not. I did not leave the school yard during recess but as soon as school was out, there I was in my Momma's lap.

From kindergarten to fifth grade I attended Ethan Allen. In sixth grade I transferred to William E Gladstone. Gladstone was my first experience of leaving the neighbor and walking a distance to school. Gladstone was also the school that my older sisters attended. During my years at Gladstone I experienced something tragic. One day there was a car accident; the car was totally smashed. After school ended, we went home only to find out that the person in the car was a neighbor who was killed instantly. I really felt sorry for the lady and her family.

At the age of 10 my Dad passed away from diabetes and heart disease. It was unusual for my Dad to be home during the day, so I tried to go into my parents' bedroom to talk to my Dad. My Mom told me that my Dad was not feeling well, and I should let him sleep. I was going to the movies and I wanted to let my Dad know. When my Mom walked away, I went into my parent's room and told my dad I was going to the movies. My Dad opened his eyes and told me to have a good time and to be good. I found out after my Dad had died and I was old enough to understand that he was in a coma and he couldn't have said anything, but he did I did. I found out that my Dad had a stroke and slipped into a coma and never regained consciousness. Now it was just me and my Mom after my Dad passed away. My Mom started working as a housekeeper cleaning rich people's home. She worked for a family in Evanston, Illinois, the Pekins family. I would go to work with my Mom sometimes and that meant taking the train. The Pekins had two children and I remember playing with their daughter, Cindy. This family owned a tailor shop on Roosevelt Road. I used to go to the store with my Mom to pick up her check and sometime drop Cindy off when she came home with my Mom.

At the age of 13 I got pregnant with my first son; the father of my son was 14 years old. Jerry was my first boyfriend and sexual experience and it resulted with me getting pregnant. A baby having a baby. One of my sisters wanted me to have an abortion but my Mom was not hearing that. My Mom told us that "she got pregnant she is going to have the baby". Thank God I had a mother who valued me getting an education because I was able to go to school during my entire pregnancy. We were supposed to be boyfriend and girlfriend, what a joke two babies not knowing the first thing about having a relationship or what sex was about. I was very immature, and I did not know I was pregnant. I only knew my period was late. I told my sister and she told my mother. My first clinic appointment, my Mom cried. Being so young I did not realize the severity of being pregnant and the obligations and responsibilities of being a mother. I had no idea and no concept of what I would be facing. This was my freshman year in high school! For freshman year I attended Family Living Center School for Pregnant Teens. This school was located on the South side of Chicago.

Snowstorm of 1967 I was pregnant with my first child. One day I was on my way to school and I saw a trail of blood leading from the sidewalk in front of our neighbor's house along the side of her house. I looked over the fence and discovered someone lying in the snow face down in the snow. I went in the house screaming for my mom. She called the police and when they arrived, they discovered it was our neighbor, Marguerite, she had been stabbed to death. That was a sight I will never forget. It was discovered that her live-in boyfriend had threatened to kill her, but it was never proven that he was her killer.

July 1967, I gave birth to my first son Derrick. It was a difficult pregnancy and birth; I went into labor on Friday and he was not born until Sunday morning. Delivered by a mid-wife on our kitchen table. Ironically, my sisters gave birth to their first born on the same table. After I gave birth the mid wife told my mom "we didn't think she was going to make it." My Mom took care of my son, bathing him, feeding him and my sister was my babysitter during the day. Mom would work, get off work come home and take care of my son until I returned from school. This arrangement worked out perfect. My sister did not work so she would babysit my son so I could go to school and my Mom could work.

My sophomore year I attended Richard T Crane High School on the Westside of Chicago. I always got good grades, but high school was not what I expected, and I had too much freedom, my Mom did not know where I was or who I was with. I cut class until my grades started failing and that brought pressure from my Mom. Richard T Crane High School was close to the Rockwell Garden Housing Project. I started smoking cigarettes daily basis and some occasional wine drinking. In my sophomore year I started hanging out in Rockwell Garden Housing Projects. My new friends went to class so that was a good thing and I started going to class as well. After school recreation included attending school dances and basketball games. That year I met a young lady named Geraldine; we called her Geri for short. Geri introduced me to her boyfriend David, and he introduced me to his brother, Melvin. Looking for love again, I got involved with someone who really did not know how to have a relationship any more than I did. After school we would go to David and Melvin's house listen to music and just hang out.

My junior year in high school I met Gwen. Gwen lived in Rockwell Garden Projects. She would come over on the weekends to my sister's house. My sister Olivia loved playing spades card game on weekends. Me and some of my friends would go over and play cards, smoke marijuana and drink wine. I introduced Gwen to Charles; Charles lived in the Abbott Housing Project. There were times when I wanted to do the high school things (going to dances, skating or just hanging with friends) and could not because I had a baby and I did not have a babysitter. Those were the times when my Mom would play the "you have a baby" card. She should have done that more often and not taken on the responsibility of raising my son.

I was seeing two guys, one lived in Rockwell Garden and the other lived around the corner from where I lived. Ronald lived around the corner and he sold weed and smoked weed. When we were together Ronald and I smoked weed, he did not drink wine, so I had that all to myself. Ronald knew his life was going nowhere with how and what he was doing. Not having a job, selling weed and he was pool hustler. So, he joined the Marines.

May 1970 my senior year I got pregnant with my second child. I joke with my son that he graduated twice from high school because when I graduated from high school, I was pregnant. My second child, Deon was born in 1971. Deon was an easy pregnancy and delivery. I would have to touch my stomach to make him move around. When I gave birth to Deon, he was born sleep. When Deon was born it was quiet, so I asked the Dr. "what is wrong with my baby? His response was "He's just sleeping."

Early summer 1971 I moved out of my mom's house into my first apartment in Rockwell Gardens. Melvin moved in with me and Deon. Derrick stayed with my Mom because she did not want him "living in the projects." During this time, my drug and drink usage was almost never.

CHAPTER 2

TOO YOUNG TO MARRY

December 1971 Melvin and I were married. We were too inexperienced and just not ready to take on the responsibility that came along with marriage. We tried to make the best of a situation that was doomed from the very beginning. I had a job and he did not, and we had mothers that did not like each other but tolerated each other. During our stay in Rockwell, Melvin and I had a lot of distractions. My In-laws lived not far from us, so Melvin spent a lot of time at their house. Melvin and I lived in Rockwell for a couple years then moved returning to the Loomis Court Projects which is located in "The Village." Looking back, that was the best move I could have made because I could work, go back to school, take care of my kids and be close to my Mom. But it was not a good move for my marriage. My husband began working at the state prison and life was good. My husband adopted Derrick so were living as a family and life was good. We enjoyed the boys and made sure that they had the best life that we could provide. Each summer we went on a family vacation to Wisconsin Dells. The boys and a couple of times other friends and their families went with us.

Melvin lost his job and things went down fast. After losing his job, he started drinking and just hanging out with my cousin who did not work either. Needless to say, the marriage ended in divorce after only 3 years. I can remember a lot of good memories. Derrick, Deon and I use to have such a good time especially having our "air band sessions" where we would listen to music and play our "air" musical instruments. We listened to all types of music, from Bach to Luther Vandross, from Traffic to Elton John. Their friends would come over and ask, "what kind of music are you listening to?" The boys would respond just as I taught them "we have culture because our Momma loves music." Music was a big thing in our house and still is today. I tried to do the best I could with what I had but always seemed to have to fall back on my Mom which was pressuring her to work harder.

I was working full time and I was a full-time college student receiving public assistance. I attended Harold Washington Community College and my major was supposed to be a Social Worker. I only started going to college so I could receive the monetary grants. It was more about money than getting an education. Not sure when I enrolled but I can tell you once I got the check I did not go back.

It got to a point that my apartment was a party apartment drinking, smoking pot, snorting cocaine and playing spades. Since this is where my roots were. I knew everybody, and everybody knew me. I started selling pot and got involved with a guy, Eddie. Eddie and his brother supplied the neighborhood with drugs, namely pot and cocaine. Eddie was the pool hustler, crap shooter and neighborhood drug dealer. It was easy for me to get involved with him and his lifestyle, because he was that "bad boy image" that I loved. To make ends meet, I started selling drugs; cocaine and weed. After selling drugs for a while I discovered I could make more money and stay at home then I could get from the college grants. Selling to the neighborhood people and using myself. I would sell to neighborhood addicts and use their drugs along with them. I was getting

Public assistance, food stamps and selling drugs. I was able to make sure that my sons had the best of everything, or so I thought. They were never neglected because of my behavior. I always made sure they had food and the best clothes money could buy. Eddie and I broke up after a short amount of time. We were still friends but not in a relationship. While Eddie and I were seeing each other his brother, Willie had a friend called Budgy, I do not know how it happened but Budgy and I started to get involved in a relationship.

December 1976, I got pregnant by Budgy. A few months after giving birth, I was offered a remodeled apartment on the Southside of Chicago, in an area still known as South Shore and I jumped at the offer. Thinking this would help me to change my life and lifestyle. Geographical change is not the answer and never the cure because wherever you go you take that same person with you. Budgy moved in with us and that did not last long. There was a lot of domestic violence, verbal and physical. A few months after moving in he moved out. His Mom lived in the Village and instead of him working or trying to find a job, he would leave my apartment and not return until late at night or the next day. With me working and taking care of the bills by myself I had enough. After one of his many trips back and forth, I told him I wanted him to move out. We got into an argument and I was holding Derron. He slapped me so hard that I dropped Derron on the floor! My impulse kicked in I picked up a knife and stabbed him. I am not proud of that moment; thank God I did not kill him. I have always been overprotective of my sons and when Derron hit the floor I saw red. Our relationship ended and I was on my own. Ronald never returned from the Marines; he settled in Richmond, Virginia. On one of his trips homes to visit his Mother, he called me and came over for a visit. It was good seeing Ronald again and I can say I wish we could have had a longstanding relationship, but it was not in God's plan.

Now I have 3 boys and we made the best of it. I started working at

WFMT Classical Radio as a secretary in the media department. By this time, the drug usage had increased and gone from snorting cocaine to freebasing. Freebasing is a form of cooking the cocaine to remove the impurities. Getting high at my desk and in the lady's bathroom freebasing cocaine and drinking. During my breaks I was chain smoking cigarettes. I did not have that job one year before I quit. Looking back, I quit because it was in the way of me using. I did not think I had a problem because I worked and was taking care of my boys.

I applied for a job training program through the neighborhood work program working for the State of Illinois. I bought my first brand new car that year; a 1976 Ford Granada. I worked for the State of Illinois Parole and Pardon Board as a file clerk and was later promoted to Secretary for the Parole and Pardon Board. I was in that position for 3 years and later transferred to the Department of Economic Security. My job at DES (Department of Economic Security) was accepting unemployment applications and making sure they were filled out so they could be processed. I started to hang out and not taking care of my business due to partying all weekend. My children were spending weekends with my Mother. I would start partying on Friday until Sunday evening when I had to pick up my kids and get ready for work that Monday. There was a dance club where I would go with friends there, we would smoke weed, take acid and drink.

At some point, I moved from the apartment in Southshore back to the Westside taking an apartment down the street from my Mom with my boys and my niece Debra.

Debra was a lot of help, but she and I did the same things, so it was more like a party relationship not a niece and aunt relationship. Considering I am only 4 years older than her; she was more like a sister. My niece gave birth to her first child, a girl Tatiana. My sons loved Tatiana like she was their sister. I received a Section 8 housing voucher which subsidized my rent and moved to Englewood neighborhood into a totally remodeled apartment and new neighborhood: Englewood. By this time, the two boys were pre-teens. I was still working for the State of Illinois DES and partying with my work buddies and someone always had something to get high on.

CHAPTER 3

MOVING WITHOUT A PURPOSE

I started going to Bob's Bar with Olivia and this is where I met my second husband Van. My sister told me when we met, this man is not for you. But I was amazed that someone like him wanted me. He was 9 years older than me, a Chicago Police Officer with a reputation of being a "bad ass." His nickname was Starsky and his partners nickname was Hutch. His bad boy image was attractive to me. After we started dating, I found out he had a girlfriend living with him. How I found out, she came to my apartment with a gun and rang the bell; my son answered the door. I still believe If I would have answered the door, I might not be here now. I called Van and he came right over, by this time his girlfriend Brenda, had ran but he caught up with her and they struggled but he took the gun from her. We broke up after that but started seeing each other again a few months later. By this time, she had moved out of his house. He and I spent a lot of time together. Derrick was in high school and Deon was graduating from elementary school on his way to high school. Derrick and Van did not get along at all. Van was always challenging him. Eventually Derrick moved back in with my Mom.

A neighbor who was the local drug dealer and I started hanging out.

She would credit me cocaine until payday. I started getting high by myself; freebasing when the boys were not around. I always thought they did not know what was going on. Deon told me after he became an adult that had he came home from school one day and he saw me using drugs and he just closed the door and pretended he didn't see me. I would lock myself up in my bedroom and get high, only coming out to check on the boys occasionally and buying more drugs. A young lady that grew up in the same neighborhood where I was born named Reynette. Reynette and I worked with at the Department of Economic Security Unemployment Office. Reynette moved into an apartment around the corner from where we lived. She and I started getting high together and partying not only at work but also when we are not working and on the weekends.

Reynette knew more people at DES (Dept of Economic Security), she introduced me to a guy named Larry. Larry sold weed and acid. That was my intro to acid tabs. Reynette and I would split a Tab soda during the day to keep us going and take No-Dose after being up all night. On the weekends we would go dancing with more friends that worked with us. Cedric and Joe also lived down the street from the office where we worked. So now we have a place to hang out especially in the wintertime when the weather was so bad. We could not hang outside because Chicago's winters can be brutal. Larry supplied us with acid and weed and we would pay him on payday for what he had given us during the week. With all this going on, my relationship with Van was on-going.

Van and I got married and we moved in with him. Moving from the neighborhood of drugs, gangs and all sorts of riff raff into one of the most prestigious neighborhoods in the city of Chicago was a big plus. Van lived in one of the most exclusive neighborhoods in Chicago, Chatham which is located on the Southside of Chicago. I gave up my apartment to live in a home in a family-oriented neighborhood. I felt the boys would benefit from this move and this marriage. Van was very controlling and mentally he controlled me. He didn't physically abuse me, but I had to account for everything I did and everywhere I went. But he gave me anything I asked for.

I found out while at work one day that one of the young men that I got high with at work lived around the corner from where I lived. He and I started hanging out at his house and doing drugs at his house whenever we could. Van was a functioning alcoholic; he worked every day but he also drank every day. By this time, we only had Deon and Derron living with us; Derrick lived with my Mom. Things increasingly got worse between Van and I due to me using drugs and Van drinking. The police department forced Van into treatment, and he decided I should go to treatment as well. I did not think I had a problem but whatever he wanted I did. As far as I know he stayed sober, but I did not. We fought and I would leave and binge and come back home. This behavior went on for a few years. A lot of times I started the fights so I could leave and use.

The next phase of my drug using, my bottom started rising. I started hanging out in the Roseland neighborhood. I would visit my sister, Earlene leave her house and get together with my nephew Darryl buy some freebase cocaine and get high with him and a friend of his named Luther who I started having a relationship with shortly after. One time Van followed me to Luther house where I was getting high, he and Luther got into a fist fight. During this time, my Mother got sick, little did I know the next year she would pass away. My Mom was diabetic, she went into a coma and never regain consciousness. God in Heaven knows I miss her!

I recall being at my mom's funeral with my boys walking into the church and being numb. My memory of my Mom services, walking down the aisle with my 3 sons and Berniece, Deon's Grandmother walking with us. Sadly, my Mom's funeral service is a blur to me. I wish I remembered and how this affected my sons. After the funeral services I went to a guy's house that I knew where to get some drugs and I got high all night.

This life led to me experiencing events in my life that I never imagined. Being arrested several times for soliciting men and trespassing, being homeless because I wanted the freedom to use, hungry because I spent all my money on drugs. Doing things, I never thought all in the name of drugs and alcohol. I slept in abandoned cars and buildings, ended up with frost bite to both of my feet but that did not stop me.

I was introduced to the neighborhood freebase cooker by his brother. This guy allowed me to live with him if I did what he wanted me to do. It got to a point that I did not care about myself or anyone else. I was considered as his main lady. Along with this title came me cleaning his house and allowing him to have other women along with me and partying. This kept me from having to go and hustle drugs and I had a place to sleep and eat. When he wanted to have other women without me being around, he would give me cocaine (freebase) and I would have to go somewhere else to get high. There were times when I would use all the drugs, he gave me, I would go back to his house and he would not let me in. Those are times I had to find somewhere to go and usually not to sleep but to get high, usually in abandoned buildings or abandoned cars. There would be times I would hang out in front of the neighborhood liquor store to get picked up by strangers who was looking to buy drugs. They would buy drugs from me and we would go to the neighborhood hotel and get high. Food was not a priority and by this time I probably didn't weigh 100 lbs.

During these times Van sent Derron to Michigan to live with his mom. He did the best he could at that time. Deon lived on the Westside with his Grandmother and attended one of the best high schools in Chicago. Deon finished college and became a professional basketball player. After my Mom's death Derrick lived on the west side and anywhere else, he could survive. Not knowing very much about how Derrick survived or where he was living at this time, he told me after my Mom passed, he had to survive the best way he could.

My niece, Deneen worked at the neighborhood church, Roseland Christian Ministry Center. My oldest sister Earlene lived around the corner from the church. I would visit my sister and she would say to me "aren't you tired? I will pray for you." I would see the pain in her face and that only gave me more reason to use and feel sorry for myself.

One day I went by to visit her and she told me Van had divorced me and threw my personal belongings into her back yard. This should have angered me, but it did not because what else was he to do. This pattern and behavior lasted for 8 years. I never imagined my life spiraling the way it did; I felt like I wanted to die.

There were times when Deon would come home during off season, and he would seek me out never judging me. When he would leave, he would always tell me "I love you Momma." On one of his trips from Spain, Deon had my now daughter-in-law Dafna with him. You would think he would have been embarrassed to introduce us, but he was not. 1995 Derron graduated from High School sad to say he had to remind me that I attended his graduation.

When this affliction called addiction started, I weighed maybe 150-160 pounds and after addiction I would be surprised if I weighed 100 lbs. soaking wet. I remember one time being held by a guy with a machete and raped. You would think that would have stopped me, but it did not because I was sick. I was going in and out of jail for soliciting and arrested for having drug paraphernalia more times than I can remember. The police knew who I was living with and they picked me up one day and wanted me to give them names of local drug dealers and I wouldn't. At that time, I had warrants for soliciting, so I was arrested and this time I did not get out. I was sentenced to 61 days in Dwight Prison. In Illinois if a conviction sentence is over 60 days the time served was 31 days. I was released right back into the place where I used.

I literally lived on the streets for the next few years using drugs, drinking and doing whatever I had to do to survive. The guy I who prepped drugs for several dealers in the neighborhood got busted and went to prison for several years. I found myself worse off than ever. I had nowhere to live and no one to turn to. So, I started hanging with the homeless and sleeping wherever I could because my focus was to not feel. This lasted for 2 years in and out of jail, being in seedy places doing seedy things.

I went by to visit my niece Deneen who worked at Roseland Christian Center because she had asked me to meet her after she got off work. Deon was in town and he wanted to see me. I went home with her, living on the streets I was dirty and hungry. I took a bath, ate and slept for 2 days. I did not realize I had slept that long. Later I found out that her children put a mirror under my nose because they thought I had died. No, I had not died I was extremely exhausted. As the saying goes in Alcoholic Anonymous "I sick and tired of being sick and tired." I didn't want to use drugs anymore, but I didn't know how to stop. Before this I recall walking down the Michigan Ave in Roseland crying, tired no sleep and hungry. I heard something or someone behind me and as I turned there was my Mother walking behind me (my Mother passed away several years before). I know that it was my Mother who was looking after me all the times I was out it the streets and it was time to change. I wanted change and I wanted it now.

CHAPTER 4

RECOVERY IS POSSIBLE

The last time I had a drink or a drug in my system was July 20, 1996. I entered treatment on July 29, 1996 after spending eight days in Cook County Jail for probation violation for soliciting and possession of drug paraphernalia. Thank God the Judge gave me time served or I could have ended up in prison. I was released on July 21, 1996. Upon my release my sons picked me up. I remember like it was yesterday. It was so quite in the car you could hear a pin drop. I felt like I had to say something, so I did. I started with "I know" and before I could say anything else, Deon said "if this is the way you want to live you need to stay away from us and my children." My sons have always respected me and never talked back to me. I knew then that they were tired and afraid for me. Usually I would come back with some smart remark. However, I knew the time had come for me to get my life in order before I lost the only people that I felt still believed in me.

I had visited Luther General Hospital some years before. My first time in treatment I went because this is what Van wanted that's why I called it "a visit." My sons drove me to Luther General Hospital where detox and in-patient was a 30 days program which included daily meetings with group counseling sessions. Upon admission I was assigned a counselor, Russ Vanoy. Russ told me that if a wanted to get sober and maintain sobriety I was going to have to change not only my way of living but also my thinking; I had to change everything. Meeting with Russ is when I realized that I had a lot of fear and it was mostly fear of the unknown. What would people think of me if they knew I had been molested as a child? Or that I searched for a father's love from every relationship I had? It was not my fault for being molested. In August of 1996, my sons, sister and niece Dashan came out to a group session with me. During that session I heard their feelings of my actions (I do not recall the conversation), I do know something was said that stuck with me, one of my sons and I don't remember which one is was said "Momma I don't want you to die."

On August 23, 1996 I was admitted in the Independent Living Program (ILP) where I shared an apartment with 2 other female patients. The complex had nine 3-bedroom apartments all furnished. Everything was provided except food. I had to get a job, so I got a job! Can you imagine how scary that was I had not worked in years! Something that I know today, God was with me all the time through the years of drug, alcohol and life abuse He never left me.

My first job interview I was hired at Jewel/Osco as a clerk/bagger making minimum wage. I was so proud of myself. I called Deon in Spain and told him I had a job. For the first time in years, my son told me "Momma I am proud of you." I am working part time and I attended mandatory meetings every day. I also attended Lutheran General Honeymooners CA meeting on Thursday and Saturday evening, and on my days off work I attended AA meetings held at Des Plaines Alcoholic Anonymous Alano Club. That summer Doc a friend of mine from the ILP Program and I attended the Marine graduation ceremony for Derron. My son had become a man and I did not recognize him. I walked right past him. That was a very memorable trip. We drove down to Tijuana and visit the Animal Zoo. My son had grown up and I had missed so much of his life.

About 4 months in ILP I got sick, I went to the doctor and I was diagnosed with fibroid tumors and surgery was needed. Thank God I came into recovery when I did. When the tumor was removed, it was the size of an orange. I feel if I were still using, I would be dead today, but God had other plans because the tumor was benign! I had to have a total hysterectomy. Six months into recovery it was time to move on. Fear based I did not want to go back to Chicago, so I moved a couple of blocks from the treatment center and ILP. During my stay at ILP we were a family. I met and became close to a guy from Rockwell Garden projects, we did not know each other back in the day but we knew the same people. Doc had been there over a year. Along with others in the house we were "family." I worked with Kim and she became my first sponsor. I met Anna at the Honeymooners CA meeting and her boyfriend lived at the house as well. Kim guided me through the twelve steps of Alcoholic Anonymous which I today thank God for her; she showed me what I needed to do to continue recovery. Kim showed me the program of recovery is simple: work the steps, go to meetings and do not use. This is a simple program for complicated people. I moved into my apartment and continued my program low and behold I was celebrating 1 year of continuous sobriety. The AA program teaches us to always remember that last drunk and keep it simple.

In 1997, I visited Deon in Malaga, Spain during his basketball season. If I wasn't sober that would have never happened. The following year I went back to Spain as well flying first class to another country and having a passport. This could have never been possible without my God and the program of recovery. I experienced being in another country, visiting places I never could have imagined. I watched my son play basketball and met people who were telling me how great he was. This trip Derron, Tatiana and my grandsons, Ryan and Dominique we all travelled to Gibraltar. During our trip there we had lots of laugh one incident that we still talk about today, while on the rock of Gibraltar a monkey ran pass Derron snatched his bag of potato chips and ran! That evening Deon, Derron and I went to a dance club, here is another funny there was lots of dancing and I love to dance during my dancing I started screaming "ow ow" and everyone on the dance floor started screaming "ow ow!" Good times and good memories

When I returned from Spain it was time to move out of ILP into my own apartment. My apartment was located down the block from ILP. I had no money so here I am depending on my Deon again. I may not have mentioned this, but my entire treatment was self-pay because I had not insurance. Deon paid for my treatment and he supplemented my stay at ILP. When I was discharged I was terrified to return to Chicago so I asked Deon if he would help to get an apartment in Des Plaines and he told me I will do whatever I can to help you as long as you stay sober. My pay did not equal to me having to buy furniture or even cover my rent, so Deon did that for me.

After years of not having Derron in my life we lived together. He was discharged from the Marines and came to live with me. It was a rocky road at first, he did not have the experience of having me in his life because addiction took me away from him at a young age. We both had to learn how to live with one another. I recall an incident where I was talking to him about something and he talked back. That is and was not acceptable, I told him "as long as you live don't you ever talk back to me! He said this is my brother's apartment not yours." After we had a cool off period, he came to me and apologized saying "Momma I am sorry I just don't want to look up and you are gone again." This still brings tears to my eyes. I told Derron, I cannot make any promises, but I am here now, and my plan is to be here forever. It was times like this that I realize just how much I had missed and couldn't get that time back, but I could make the coming days better if I didn't use.

I was promoted to full time cashier and Scan Coordinator Assistant. The Scan Coordinator, Maryanne was a short Italian lady that loved me, and she taught me everything she knew about the position. Maryanne passed a few months later and I was promoted to Scan Coordinator. This job gave me the confidence that I had lost to addiction. I felt my worth had returned. Being around people who trusted me, who looked up and trusted me. That feeling of self- worth was returning. Still attending meetings, attending conferences, I was loving myself and life.

Derron turned 21 years old and we had a birthday party for him at my apartment. Deon, several friends, family, Doc and I played cards ate birthday cake. My Niece, Debra had purchased some beer and Derron went berserk "get that out of here"!" He was afraid I was going to drink. After seeing his reaction, I assured him I didn't want and wasn't going to drink and that it was okay if anyone else wanted to.

In 1999 I had the blessing of another overseas trip to the Canary Islands and the biggest blessing was I met my granddaughter, my Little Princess, Gabby. This trip was one that I will always cherish, I was able to be in sobriety, hold my granddaughter and spend precious time with Deon, Dafna and their new baby girl, Gabrielle Bernice.

Upon my return from vacation, Derron moved into his own apartment. He would visit me every day and we would just talk about any and everything. The guy that I lived with in Roseland, Melvin (not my ex-husband) was released from prison and came to visit me. He told me he wanted a different life and he did not want to go back to prison. I allowed him to move in with me trying to help him like I had been helped. That did not last very long. His Mom lived in Roseland so his excuse to return for a visit was legitimate. During one of his visits he stayed away the entire weekend. I had to set priorities; my sobriety or my relationship with him. My sobriety won because I knew that he had used drugs and if I wanted to stay sober, I had to cut ties, so I did.

July 2000 was the Cocaine Anonymous convention in Scottsdale, Arizona. Anna and I were roommates. I met some awesome people including Ginny (my future Sponsor). I recall sitting on the patio at the hotel in Scottsdale looking up at the sky. This night the sky was full of stars. I was looking up and I said, "God I would really love to live here." We returned to Illinois from the convention and a couple of months later the Osco

Manager called me into his office and asked if I wanted to apply for a promotion to Corporate located in Scottsdale, Arizona! I was flabbergasted to say the least. Of course, I said yes. I applied and was offered the position! I had to report by October 1st. This was another God moment. While I was in Arizona, Ginny told me if I were ever in Arizona again to call her. I called Ginny told her what happened, and she offered to help me find an apartment. I called my sons and told them what happened.

August 2000, I flew back to Arizona. Ginny met me at Sky Harbor Airport, and she drove me to an apartment complex in Scottsdale. I completed the rental application, leased an apartment and went back to the hotel. This was on a Saturday, not having anything to do I went to the hotel desk and asked if there was some place close that I could go and just spend a little time because my flight was not leaving until the next morning. The front desk clerk told me they had a shuttle that would take me over to Casino Arizona. In Illinois the casinos were boats; this one was a tent. I walked in and a machine that I played back in Illinois was there in front of me, Sizzling 7's! I inserted a $20 and pulled the lever a couple of times and hit the red sizzling 7's which paid $2400. I didn't say this earlier, but I was trying to figure out how I was going to make this relocation because I didn't have any savings. However, God's plan is always better than our plans. I went back to Des Plaines and started scheduling the move from Illinois to Arizona. The cost of reserving the moving truck was $1200. My winnings from the casino covered my moving expenses. There He is again, God doing for me what I could not do for myself.

My friends and store employees gave me a going away party. I am looking at the clock they give me right now "Joanna Johnson best of luck Osco #37." My sister Earlene, my niece Pam, Lon Pam's son, DaShan my niece (God rest her soul) attended the dinner party that evening along with Derron and his girlfriend. While working at Osco I met a lot of people one of them is Diana who is still in my life today and she calls me "Momma Jo." She relocated to Arizona a couple of years after me. Anna did the road trip with me moving to Arizona. Earlier that year Deon had purchased me a silver Rodeo. Anna and I had a ball driving across country, I still have the pictures from the drive.

CHAPTER 5

New Life

We arrived in Arizona September 25, 2000. I moved into my apartment in Scottsdale, Arizona 56th St and Bell. I jumped right into the program. I called Ginny and she picked me up and we drove to my first CA meeting in Arizona "Saturday Night Live" which was located at a hospital in Tempe, AZ. I met a few members and my recovery circle grew in leaps and bounds. That is what I love about recovery we are all here with a singleness of purpose. Members who have stuck around for some time know what I mean. I attended AA meetings in Scottsdale at the Alano Club met others addicts and alcoholics from other fellowships who earned their seats. What I mean by "earned their seats" we hit our bottom and made a conscious decision to give recovery a try. There I met a young man Ken, who introduced me to Crossroads a halfway house in Phoenix that held CA meetings. So here I am new to Arizona, but I had an abundance of people I could call "friends."

I worked in Scottsdale at Osco Corporate office, in my office were four other women and the Office Manager. I worked 8:30am to 5pm with a 1-hour lunch. I was sitting outside in the month of October, sleeveless. I remember one of the ladies telling me this time next year you will be wearing a jacket or sweater like we are. I could not phantom that coming from Chicago! No wind? Come on! Well they were right the next winter was different, I was an Arizonian, jacket, long pants and if the temperature dropped below 70 degrees I would be freezing.

I would go to Ken's on the weekend and sometimes he would come to my apartment and we would hang out. That eventually developed into a relationship. Later the coming year Ken moved to Ahwatukee and a few months later I gave up my apartment in Scottsdale and moved to Ahwatukee. Living in the same complex was not a good idea because Ken had started seeing another girl in the program and me at the same time. I showed up a Ken's one evening uninvited and he was entertaining his other girlfriend. The relationship ended in a big fight and the loss of a friendship with Ken.

My office was in Scottsdale and I was living in Ahwatukee which was about a 1-hour drive (30 mins there and 30 mins home). I recall getting to work September 11, 2001, and Janice one of the ladies that I worked with had a small television on her desk and everyone in our office was standing around her desk. I walked over and asked what was going on and to my surprise the twin towers were being bombed. We all know what happened that day a disaster we will never forget. Seeing the towers go down one at a time was devasting to say the least.

Later, that year, I was talking to DJ and telling her about my drive. She suggested that I apply for the management training program which I did. What was nice about Osco Corporate at that time was they promoted from within. I completed the program and was assigned an assistant manager position in Scottsdale at the Hayden and Shea store. From there I was transferred to the Ahwatukee store which was located on Ray and 50th St Phoenix. I completed my training there and was transferred to the Mesa store located on Southern and Dobson.

Still living in Ahwatukee I decided to step out in faith and purchase my first home. I applied and was approved for a mortgage loan!! Six years clean and sober in recovery, managing a drug store, owning a car and buying my first home. I never imagined my life being what it was and where I was. Jenny, a friend from one of the meetings I attended, was living on Dobson and Main and I was driving to visit her. I saw a for sale sign hanging over this block wall of townhomes. I called the number, previewed the townhome and in 30 days that home was mine. I had purchased my first home. Life was good! I was still attending my meetings, sponsoring ladies in recovery, working and coming home to my home. I started attending a meeting in Mesa with Erica and Jenny. They introduced me to a women's halfway house called Angel House. It was owned and operated by Mark and Sarah Partridge. Erica, Jenny and I would lead 12 step meetings for the ladies that lived there. I sponsored women and Yolanda and Carmen were my first sponsee's in Arizona. 12 Step sponsorship is a big deal! I was able to help other women in recovery the way I was helped. Helping them to live life on life terms, studying the big book of Alcoholics Anonymous and working the 12 steps. Another meeting that I attended was another women's halfway house located in Mesa. There I sponsored as well and had the pleasure of sponsoring a young lady by the name of Mona. Mona and I told each other our story and realized we had so much in common, Mona had three sons and was married. She abandoned her family to use drugs just like I had. In the program of recovery, you learn to not look for differences in people and sponsors look for similarities.

My first year of living in Arizona I met Mischa and we became good friends; we were more like sisters. Mischa passed in 2018; God do I miss her. When Mischa and I met, she was living in Scottsdale. A few years later, Mischa moved across from my townhome. We would get together and have cookouts, Sunday dinners together, and of course go to the casino sometimes. Her daughters still to this day call me Auntie. Mischa worked in the medical field night shifts. She would ask me to keep an eye on the girls from there we developed a Auntie/Niece relationship.

I transferred to the Tempe Osco located on Baseline and Kyrene. I really enjoyed that store, but the manager was never around, so I was more of a manager than assistant manager. But that did not bother me and the gang (as I called the clerks). We worked together to make that store more profitable than it had ever been. Small store, small staff and it worked until one morning I was opening the store and I got this eerie feeling that something was not right. I opened the front door and the alarm did not beep so instead of going in the back- storage room as I did day after day, I called the police. When the officers arrived, we went in the back of the store together and the delivery back door was ajar. My usual method was to enter the front, hit the alarm pad to deactivate the alarm and walk straight to the back room. Thank God again He was watching over me. It was concluded that it had to be an employee who was a part of the burglary, but it was never proven. I enjoyed what I did and the people that I worked with. I have found in my life that it is much easier to go with the flow than to fight against the grain. So to accuse someone without proof was not possible, there were no cameras in the backroom and since nothing was missing Coming from where I was 10 years ago to where I was then was no more than a blessing it was a miracle.

A couple of years after I had purchased my home, I received a call from my grandson, Ryan's mom Ronda that they were coming to Arizona for a visit. That was a welcomed call, so I contacted my son, Don and he also felt that was a good idea. While visiting she expressed that she was considering relocating as well. Upon their arrival we decided to take a road trip and I had vacation time. We drove to Anaheim, CA to Disneyland. That was my first trip to Disneyland and to travel with my grandson, I was in heaven. We stayed at the Disney Hotel (wow if you ever have a chance to stay there please do so). We stayed there for four days enjoying each other and I was being a kid along with my grandson. Ronda and Ryan returned to Indiana but returned shortly and made Arizona their new home. It was an idea arrangement too because I got a chance to spend time with my grandson and get to know him better. I also discovered that my grandson's mom had some issues, so I was able to give him some much-needed attention as well.

I transferred to a store closer to home which was the Albertson/Osco located in Mesa on Dobson and Baseline. Working at that location I met some nice people and the manager allowed me to work daytime hours and a regular schedule. I was still attending 12 step meetings, sponsoring women and really enjoying life. That year 2004, Deon and Dafna had their 2nd child, Liel. I was not able to travel to Tel Aviv that year. Just starting a new position, I was not able to take a trip overseas, but when I saw her pictures, she looked just like Deon when he was born.

In 2004 when the housing market was starting to rise, Ronda came up with the idea that we go into the real estate business together. She said we would take real estate courses and start a business. I took real estate classes at Mesa Community College in the evening 3 times a week and still worked fulltime at the store. The real estate course was a 6-month course. My grandson's mom did not hold up her end of the arrangement, but I did. While taking classes I interviewed with Real Estate Firm that I am still with today. Terri was the Manager and she allowed me to attend the Tuesday office meetings until I finished my classes and pass the real estate to be a licensed Realtor in Arizona.

I closed my 401k with Albertson's and started my real estate business. My first year in real estate was quite fulfilling financially so I was able to resign from Albertson and pursue real estate full time. I was still active in the 12 step programs of Alcoholic Anonymous and Cocaine Anonymous, attending meetings, visiting halfway houses and sponsoring women in recovery. My first real estate transaction came about from floor time one Saturday morning (floor time is after hours or weekend coverage when the realtor takes weekend calls and office walk in's). A guy walked into the office accompanied by his two small sons stating, "I want to sell my house." Thank God that day Nancy another realtor was in the office. I am so thankful for Nancy because I did not have a clue what to do first. She walked me through taking the listing and getting the paperwork processed. I want to add this is the year I stopped smoking cigarettes, living in Arizona and smoking just don't mix.

I wanted to remodel my townhome that I was so proud of. I called a friend in the recovery program that owned a home remodel business named Kevin (may I add not my husband). Kevin came over and gave me an estimate. When he returned to start the job, he had 3 workers with him. One of the workers name Dante, we started talking. I with years of sobriety, him being what we call in the program a "newcomer" was not a good thing. The program of recovery states that it is not suggested that you get into a relationship in the first year of sobriety because you can take the focus off sobriety and start focusing on the relationship. There have been relationships that last but not many. Take this time to learn who you are and learn to love yourself. We only dated for a few months before he relapsed, that should have been enough for me, but it was not. A couple of times he was arrested during one of his many binges. Dante was arrested on a warrant and he served a few months in Maricopa County Jail. Before he was sentenced, we had talked about getting married. After his release we were married in December of 2005, but Dante just could not stay sober. He had many relapses and many promises to stay sober. After one relapse he went back into a halfway house for a while, but I allowed him to return home when I should have insisted that he stayed in the halfway house.

In 2006 Derron married Dawn, Dante and I attended their wedding in Chicago. Dante was so paranoid that he accused me of flirting with Derron's friend. I never told anyone about this, but I actually had to take him to the side and let him know he was starting to cause a scene at my son's wedding. Dante would go on a drug binge and show up at my office asking for money so he could use more drugs. I had enough when I found a crack pipe in my house! I asked him to leave and he would not, so I called the police. When they arrived, I could not believe what the police said. Because we were married, they would not escort him away from my home. He did eventually leave for a couple of days and again I let him come back in. After months of the back and forth I finally told my sons what was happening. Dante told me during a normal conversation "if I can't have you, I will kill you and then kill myself." That scared the crap out of me, it took me back to when my Mom friend and neighbor Marguerite was killed and the person that killed her was never prosecuted.

January 9, 2006 Daniel Micah Thomas was born To Derrick and Tonika. By this time Dante was stalking me. Mischa would call me and tell me she saw him at my back-yard gate. March of 2006 Tonika and Daniel came down for a visit. I was afraid for them to come but I was more afraid to tell me family what was happening. I had no choice. I finally had to tell my sons what was going on.

Deon, Derrick and Derron decided that Derrick should move to Arizona; my sons were afraid for me. Derrick moved to Arizona. I really didn't want to involve my family, but I had to at this point. The office where I practiced real estate was not far from where I lived. One day Dante showed up there and I had to take out an order of protection on him. He would call me, and I would just hang up. Up to this point I have never been afraid for my life, but now I was. He asked if we could meet somewhere and I agreed. I met him at a restaurant in Mesa. I was able to tell him that my son was now living with me and I also told him that if he loved me, he would leave me alone. I do not know whether it's because I told him my 6'5" close to 300 lbs. son lived with me or that if he loved me, he would leave me alone. It is probably because he did not want to have a confrontation with my son. I divorced Dante in December of 2006.

Derron and Dawn had a baby, Sophia Elnora. I was there in the delivery room when she was born. Here is another gift of sobriety being there when my youngest son's first and only child was born. I look back on my life and I know that this was God's plan all the time and that I had to live through what I did to enjoy what I have now. Sophia was born on

January 6, 2007. Derrick had another son that year Joshua, who was born on December 28, 2007 with his girlfriend at that time, Shan. Shan had 3 other children who still to this day call me Granma. I got my focus back after being in another abusive relationship. I made a conscience decision to focus on my recovery, my family and my business.

CHAPTER 6

FINDING MY NICHE

Being in the field of real estate you meet many people and during my years I have to say I have met the best. Especially fellow realtors and managers. The real estate office where I worked in Mesa was home to me and the agents there, were family. One of the agents met her now husband on Craigslist and she had mentioned to me about placing a dating ad on the site. That is no longer an option today because of the Craigslist killer. I went on the site and was reading some of the ads but was too afraid to post one, but I did respond to one which read "single white male 49 seeks single black female." I responded and a couple of days later I received a response. I must tell you that scared the crap out of me! After dealing with what I had a few months before, suddenly this did not sound like a good idea. I did not respond until a couple of weeks later to the email. I started with "are you still hoping to meet someone?"

A few hours later I got a response "yes, I have been on a couple of dates but nothing good." I thought maybe I need to give this guy a chance, so we arranged for him to pick me up for dinner. Mischa was living across from me, so she was my look out. When he pulled up, she called "girl he is driving a sports car and he is cute." He rang the doorbell and I opened the door. Do not ask me why I did this, but I put the biggest kiss on him, and wow could he kiss! He came in we talked for a while and decided to have dinner at the Casino. We had dinner and we played slots for a little while. He dropped me back at home and of course Misha and I had to discuss the evening events. Mischa told me after I told her how nice this guy was, how polite and respectful he was her response was "you are going to marry him." My response was I don't think so; we can be friends. We ended up going on a couple of dates, spending time together and enjoying each other's company. I invited him to a sober dance, and we had a ball. At that time, I had a couple of sponsee's tell me "he is good for you."

Our first date was August 16, 2008 and we have been together ever since. I had planned a trip to Hawaii that September and I asked Kevin if he wanted to go and he said yes. I can tell you I have never had someone to treat me the way he has and still does to this day. A couple of months after our vacation he had a business trip to San Francisco, so I drove him to the airport upon his return he gave me this gold trimmed vase of the San Francisco bridge, I still have that vase today.

Kevin's son, K2 is in a band called "The Woovs." Kevin played a CD for me and dedicated a song to me titled "I Don't Mind," that is still our song today. I made a scrap book of our first year together of all the events we attended together and with others. We did a trip to Chicago and Ohio. He met my sons and I met his daughter and son. The following year was tragic for him, he lost his Dad. On the bright side his Mom came out for a visit and I made dinner for the two of them. That was a big step in our relationship. The following year we decided to move in together. I sold my townhome and he gave up his apartment. We moved to Ahwatukee in 2009 and his Mom moved in with us. Not having enough room, we eventually moved to South Mountain and after a brief time his Mom decided to move back to their hometown, so he and I decided to downsize. Also, in 2009 our daughter, Kristian gave birth to her first child,

Johnathan, and we travelled to Ohio for his birth. That was truly a special occasion being with Kevin and experiencing the birth of his first grandchild was all so gratifying.

We love to travel and being a realtor allows me to do that. When you meet your soulmate, you will know it. We have so much in common and love doing a lot of the same things. We planned many vacations together and cruising is our favorite. In 2011 and 2012 we cruised and on the cruise in 2012 we planned a 13-day Mediterranean cruise.

In January 2013 while in bed Kevin woke me up and said, "when I lay down, I can't breathe." A couple of days after that he had a doctor's appointment for a stress test. After waiting for about half an hour the doctor came out and told me he needs to be admitted right away to the hospital. I offered to drive him to the hospital, which was directly across the street, the doctor responded that we need to transport him by ambulance and that I could meet him over there. When I arrived, I was sitting in the emergency waiting room when I was approached by a nurse who directed me to go to the cardiology floor. When I arrived there the doctor came out and told me he had a heart attack and was going to surgery. My response was OMG how I am going to tell his Mother and his children this! Thankfully, the surgery went well! He had to have a stint put in his right artery which had 98% blockage. Later, after speaking with him and the doctor he had more than one heart attack that weekend. With medical technology today, Kevin's recovery involved being home for a few days and back to work. But while being hospitalized I was there every day and we talked several times during the day.

May 2013, we went on a 13-day Mediterranean cruise and he proposed to me. Kevin told me that he thought a lot about our relationship when he was in the hospital. He asked himself "what are you waiting for I need to ask her to marry me." That was the most amazing cruise I have ever been on and I have cruised a lot in my time. The night he proposed we had a 12 or 13 course meal each including wine (none for me I had iced tea). It was called the Captain's Table, and after the meal there were after dinner cocktails in the veranda of the ship. He got down on one knee and asked me to marry him. One of the guests that attended the dinner looks at me and said, "honey if you say no, I will marry him!" We all laughed!! One of the ship guests that was not a part of our dinner sent us over an expensive bottle of champagne which we shared with our party.

We arrived in Vegas that Thursday evening, January 7, 2014, for our Bachelor/Bachelorette party on January 8th. The following day, our wedding was like a dream come true. I walked down the aisle with my youngest son, Derron giving me away to my soulmate. Our ceremony was like a fairytale. My friend for 60 years, Diane and my next-door neighbor, Dede were my maids of honor. Kevin's best friend Marty was Kevin's best man and God rest her soul my niece Deneen was our ring bearer. With other friends and family looking on, it was a blessing. January 9th is his birthday and we were married on January 10th and my birthday is January 11th! He calls these dates his "trifecta."

November of 2014 I was diagnosed with breast cancer that was truly a blow that threw us for a loop. How could this be?! We are just starting to build our life together and now this. My faith in God is so strong I knew that He had not brought me this far to take me away. I never knew at that time what Kevin was thinking because we never talked about it. There were days when I wanted to just break down and cry, but I did not. I remembered that God was in charge. After all the preparation, I had surgery in March of 2015. I had to have another surgery in the incision because the cancer was still there. In a weeks' time I had surgery twice. After surgery I had radiation twice a week for one week. I would have out-patient radiation treatment in the morning and go to my office afterwards and back in the evening for the second round of treatment then home. I will always remember that final treatment. That was the day that I broke down and cried until I could not cry anymore and then I slept for two days. I was exhausted. My heart goes out to any and everyone who has this battle behind them or in front of them. I really do not like using this word, but I hate cancer! I have lost loved ones to this horrible disease and I know countless others who have lost loved ones as well.

As you all know by now, he is my one and only, Kevin. Kevin and I have had a bond since day one and it is unshakeable. The time that we came into each other's live could have only been planned by God himself. Kevin moved from his hometown where he had been his entire life to San Francisco. I moved from my hometown to Phoenix where I had lived my entire live. After divorce we both were involved in dysfunctional relationships. We talk about this often today, that God had a plan for us to meet and at the right time. What we have today is amazing and could only have been planned by God.

I started real estate in 2005 and earning the "Rookie of the Year" award in my first year of business. Since 2007 I have been awarded "Excellence in Customer Service."2019 I earned an award that I said from day one I would earn, and I did through the Grace of God. I received a Kachina! This award is given to Agents who have excelled their business to extreme heights. Many more awards I have received but these three for me are the most important. What that means to me is that I treat others the way they want to be treated.

I have made countless number of friends in the program of Alcoholic Anonymous and Cocaine Anonymous. Through fellowship of these dynamic programs of recovery, I have accumulated over 23 years of sobriety and it is by the grace of God that I don't feel the need to numb myself. I have feelings today that are mine and they are legitimate. I have been awarded a new life because I made a very conscience decision years ago that I am not alone. My past is my past and it has made me the person that I am today. No need to be ashamed of what was because God has forgiven me, and I have forgiven myself. July 21, 2020, 24 years I have been sober and that is how long I abused my mind, body and soul with chemicals.

Living a sober live I have also been blessed with being introduced to my other Grandchildren: Laderrick, Darron, Tara and Janiya. Here's another miracle Laderrick and Tara have children, that makes me a Great-Grandmother!

If God is willing and I know that He is, if I remember one day at a time is all I have, continue to do what I have been doing, I am guaranteed another day of sobriety.

CHAPTER 7

MY TESTIMONY

Deon suggested years ago that I need to write a book because I could save so many people. I believed that then and I believe that now. You see what has transpired in my life has been what we call in Alcoholic Anonymous a "spiritual experience and a spiritual awakening." I want to also note willingness, honesty and open mindedness are the essentials of recovery. For years I lied to myself therefore I could not be honest with others. Coming into recovery today my life is an open book. I have no problem with saying that I am a recovering alcoholic and addict. I find it so easy today to be kind to others, to help others and by no means am I any better than anyone else. Life has taught me a serious lesson that if I don't continue to do what I did to get here in my life I can soon return to that life of misery. How it works from the big book of Alcoholics Anonymous tells us that "rarely have we seen a person fail who has thoroughly followed our path those who do not recover are those who cannot and will not be completely honest with themselves" and "self-will" will get me drunk. My life is running by the will of my Higher

Power whom I choose to call "God." See with Him I cannot go wrong. Born and raised in the city of Chicago in the 1950's I experienced live not knowing a thing about racism, bigotry, hate, drug abuse or fear. I was taught that we are all God's child and always to love others. Life has taught me, that the world does not owe me anything. Becoming who I am today took a lot of hard knocks, life experiences and pain. I am where I am today because I choose to change and never look back. To always remember where I came from and who should get the honor. I give all I have and all I am to my Higher Power, who I choose to call God. His is the God of my understanding. Today I love life and what I have simply because I chose not to give up."

Each morning I start my day off by praying and asking God to lead me through the day and show me how I can be of service to Him and my Fellow. I read two meditation books "24 Hours a Day" Author, Hazelden and "Each Day a New Beginning Daily Meditation for Women" Author Hazelden. I also read "Our Daily Bread" distributed by Our Daily Bread Ministries and a Chapter from the Bible. This has been my routine for 23 years and I will continue to do it all the days of my life.

I know recovery is possible, if you read this book from the beginning to now, you know recovery is possible. I do not attend as many meetings as I should, but I stay in contact with God daily. I am not cured, nor will I ever be. I hope that this book has done what it was intended to, show you that you can do it too.

JOANNA SIRAVO-HAMRIC

I CLIMBED OUT OF THE BELLY OF THE BEAST

6

I CLIMBED OUT OF THE BELLY OF THE BEAST

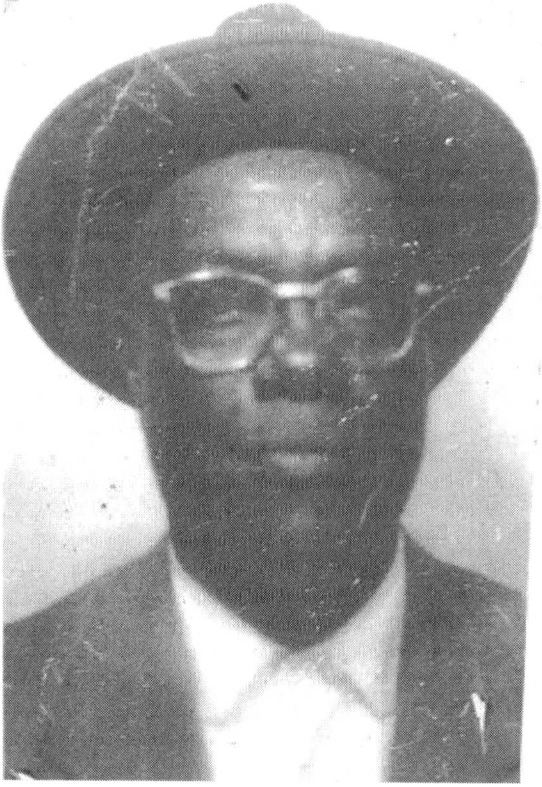

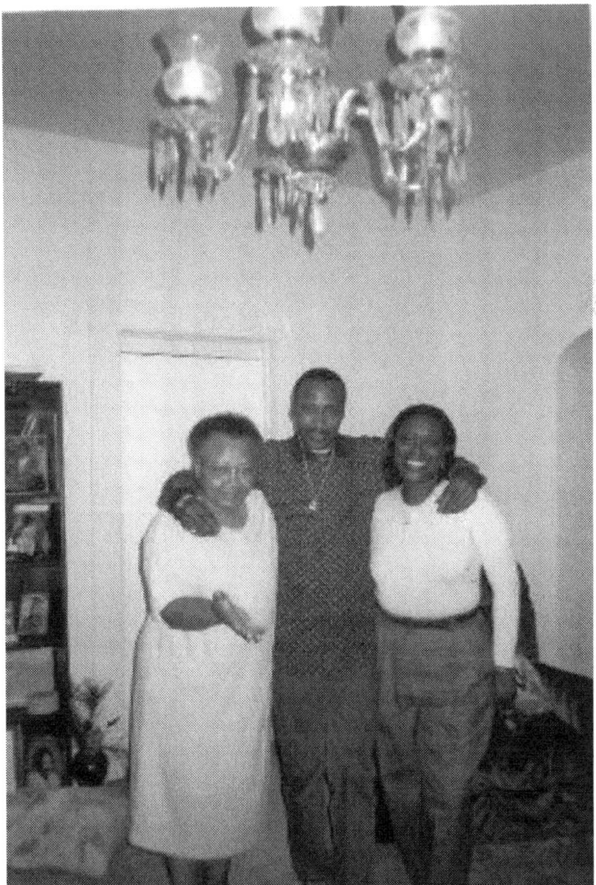

JOANNA SIRAVO-HAMRIC

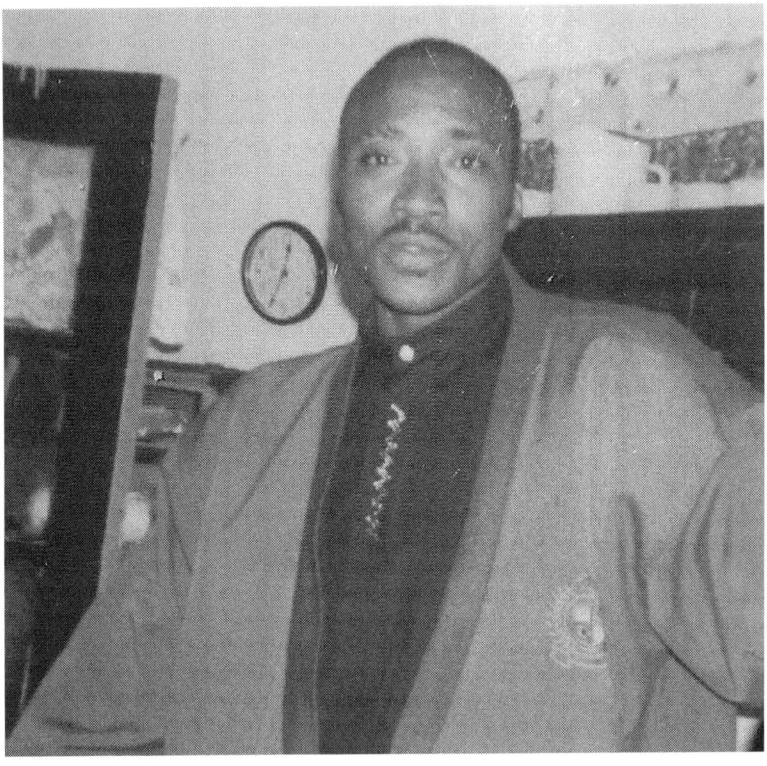

JOANNA SIRAVO-HAMRIC

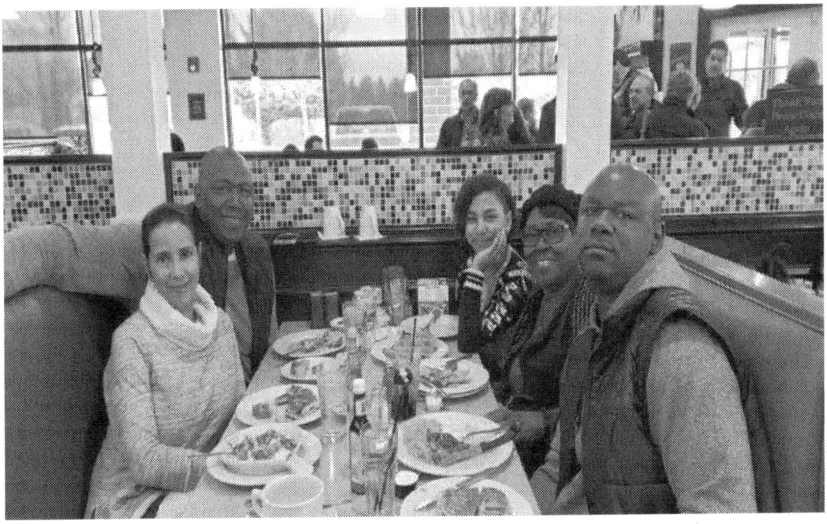

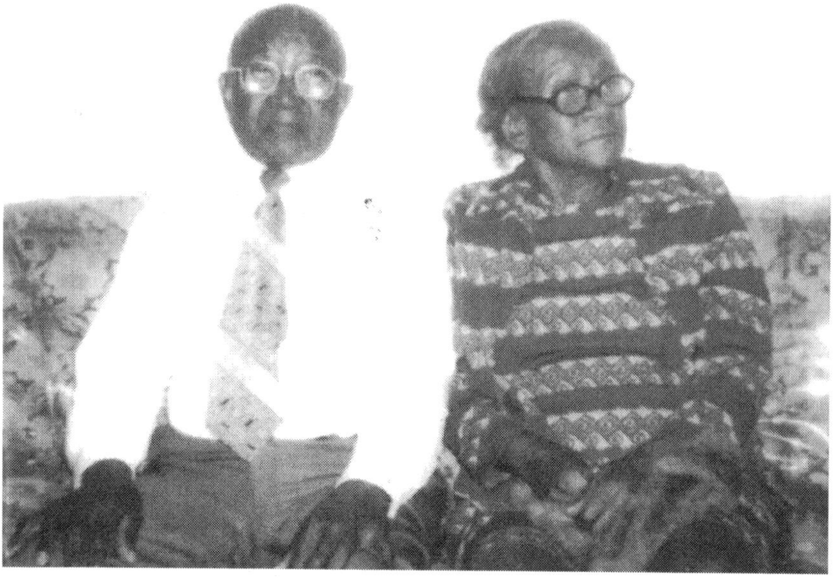

I CLIMBED OUT OF THE BELLY OF THE BEAST

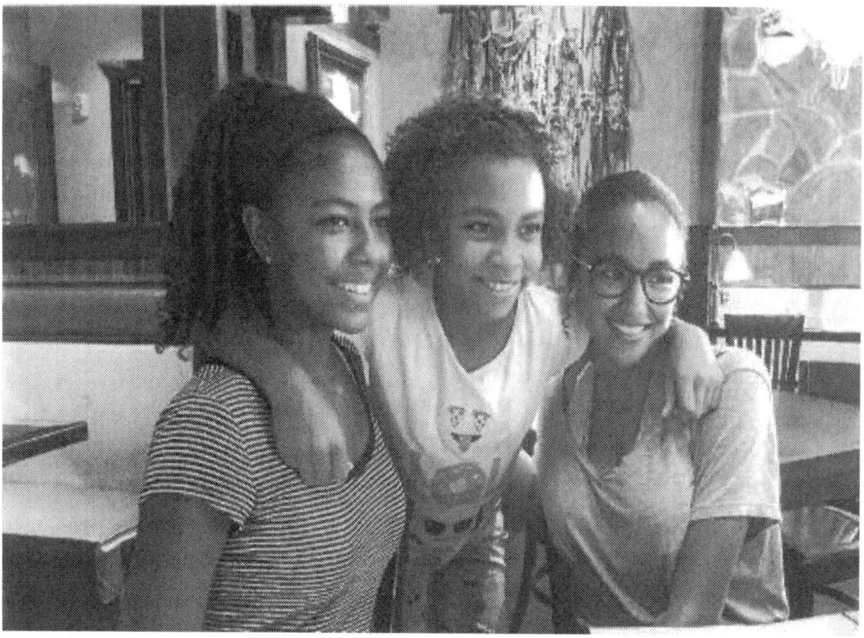

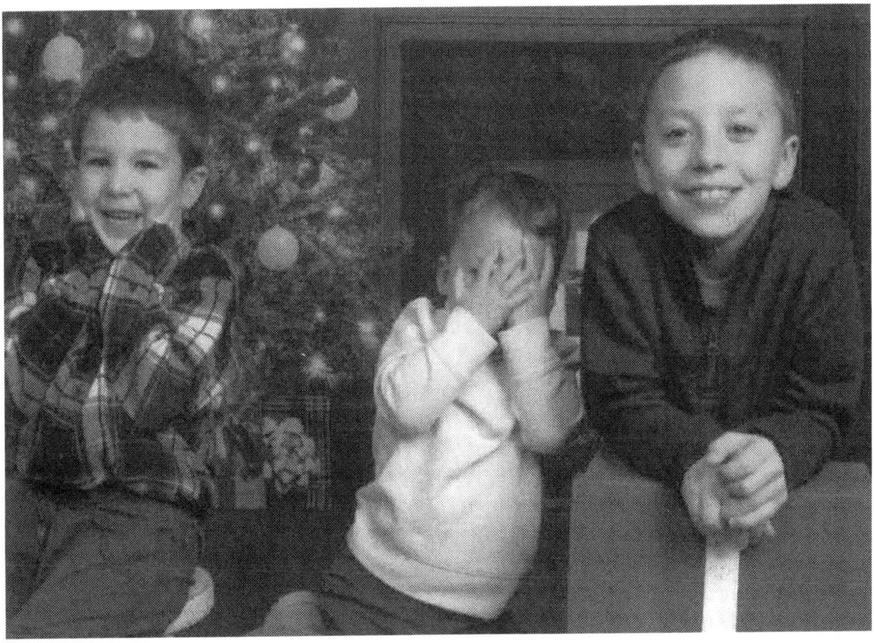

JOANNA SIRAVO-HAMRIC

#Because I have a Black Son ♥

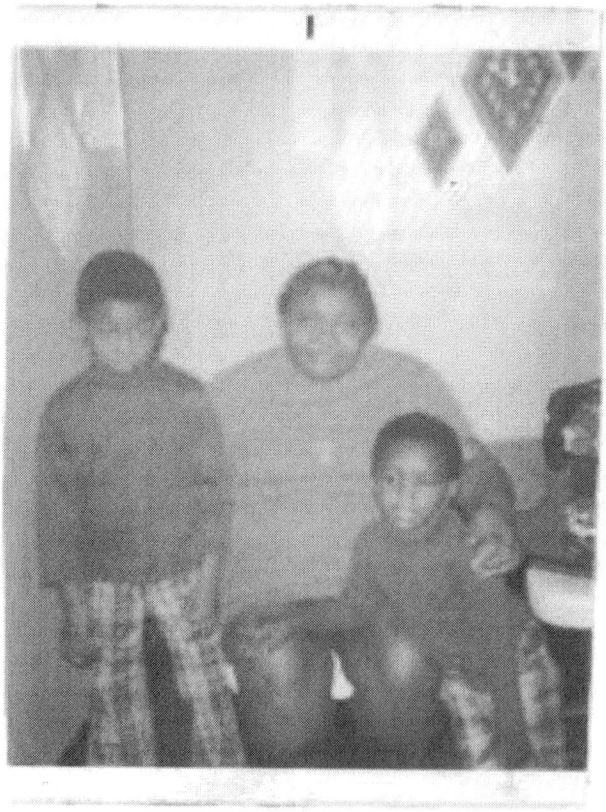

I CLIMBED OUT OF THE BELLY OF THE BEAST

JOANNA SIRAVO-HAMRIC

I CLIMBED OUT OF THE BELLY OF THE BEAST

JOANNA SIRAVO-HAMRIC

I CLIMBED OUT OF THE BELLY OF THE BEAST

JOANNA SIRAVO-HAMRIC

I CLIMBED OUT OF THE BELLY OF THE BEAST

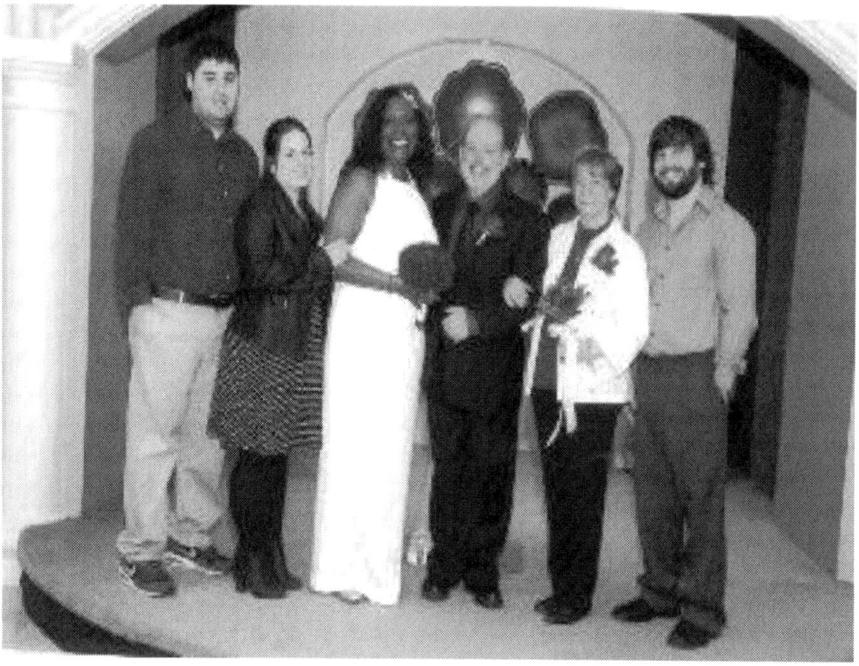

I CLIMBED OUT OF THE BELLY OF THE BEAST

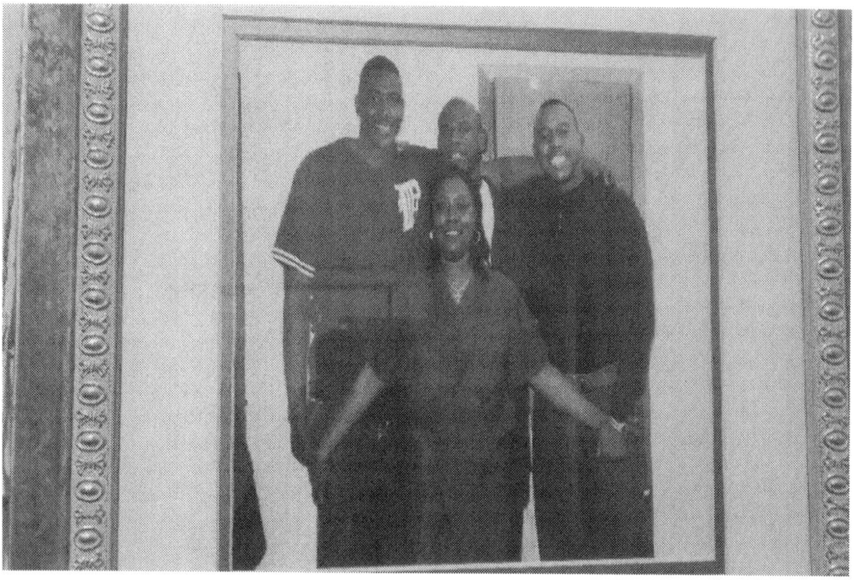

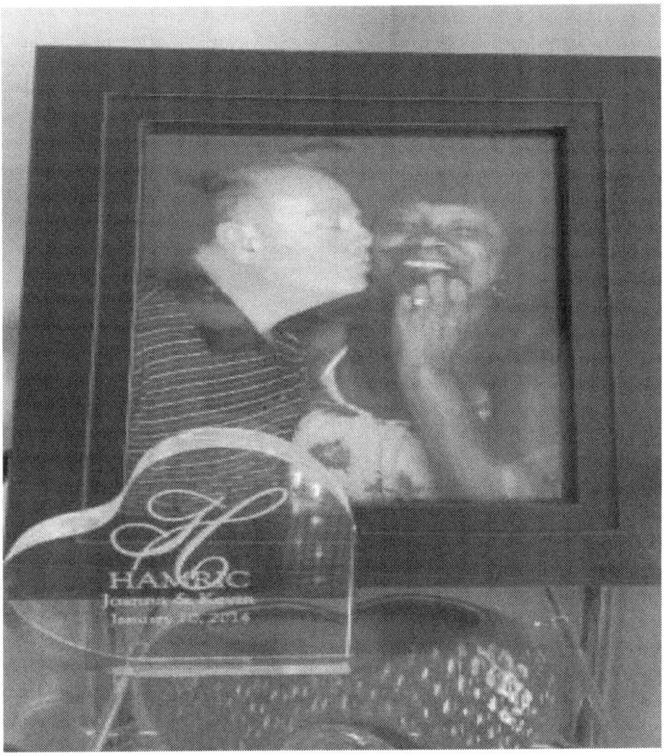

ABOUT THE AUTHOR

Joanna Siravo-Hamric has recovered from over two decades of alcohol abuse, drug abuse, domestic violence and homelessness. She is originally from Chicago, Illinois now living in Phoenix, Arizona with her Husband of six years, Kevin. Owner / President of a successful and profitable residential real estate business for 15 years with the same Real Estate Firm.

Her memoir covers the abuse and life choices as they occurred covering decades of abuse until now, her life as a recovered addict and alcoholic. She has not had a drink or drug since July 21, 1996. She has recovered from a hopeless state of mind and body.

Her reason for writing this memoir is that she can be an example to someone that they are worthy of recovery. If just one live is saved her mission has been accomplished.

Made in the USA
Middletown, DE
18 October 2022